NO SAILING WAITS

AND OTHER FERRY TALES

NO SAILING WAITS AND OTHER FERRY TALES

30 Years of BC Ferries Cartoons

ADRIAN RAESIDE

Harbour Publishing

Nobody, just nobody, escapes the ferry lineup.

July 2007, BCF announces plans to profile patrons with complaints about ferry service.

October 2005, BCF announces tightened security at terminals—specifically Horseshoe Bay, where passengers can leave the terminal to buy takeout in nearby Horseshoe Bay village.

After privatization in 2003, BCF management improved frills but not basics.

December 2011, Mike Corrigan, the new CEO of BC Ferries, arrives on the job at the same time as a ferry slams into the dock in another of what were politely called "hard landings."

It seemed odd that Victoria's 2008 Tall Ships Festival would feature a faux pirate show when we had our very own homegrown pirates sailing BC waters.

FERRY LINEUPS—OR WHERE I SPENT MY LONG WEEKEND

If you're reading this book (and hopefully you bought it and aren't just sitting in a comfy chair in the bookstore flipping through the pages) you've probably experienced a two-sailing wait—or worse. Nothing beats arriving at the ticket booth one nanosecond after the cut-off to buy tickets. You can avoid that misery by paying for a reservation, speeding past the long lineup to be among the first to board the ferry—unless you arrive at the ticket booth to claim your reservation one nanosecond after the 30-minute cutoff. Not only are you now stuck in a two-sailing wait, you're also out the cost of the reservation and the dog just threw up on your mother-in-law.

January 2012, there is talk of charging extra to those passengers who choose not to make a reservation.

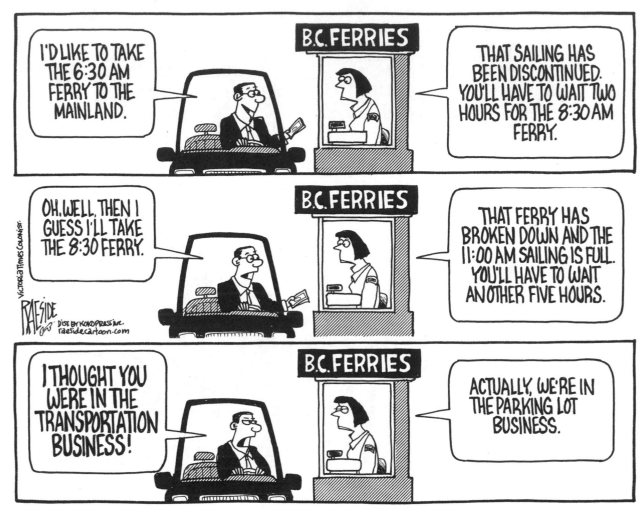

Next, parking meters . . .

Putting wait times to constructive use . . .

Experts have long been puzzled by the absence of grizzly bears on Vancouver Island. Ferry passengers knew otherwise . . .

January 2009, BCF announces $5.6 million in security enhancements.

The thrill of a ferry voyage wore thin as the lineups lengthened.

ADVENTURES IN CATERING— THE SUNSHINE BREAKFAST

For those who never had the pleasure of sitting down to a Sunshine Breakfast, the best way to describe it is that it was the gastric equivalent of a flogging. Supposedly it contained eggs, but I'm not sure any chickens were ever involved in its manufacture. It made antacid manufacturers very happy and provided me with numerous cartoon opportunities. Sadly for me, BC Ferries pulled it from the menu a few years ago, something for which I feel my numerous cartoons on the subject may have played a small part.

1998, residents living near the Swartz Bay terminal complained about the noise from departing ferries.

A union negotiating tactic hits local business hard.

There were some things even a seagull wouldn't do.

With the closure of Vancouver Island poultry processing plants, island chickens were shipped to the mainland.

April 2000, BCF is criticized over pigeon control measures at Swartz Bay. Where's PETA when you need them?

Ferry crews are trained to deal with any calamity. Well, almost any . . .

In 2005, tired of complaints about substandard food, BC hospitals outsourced catering.

The proverbial silver lining in every cloud.

The numerous crab traps littering the coast proved to be a hazard to both ferries—and crab fishermen.

The 1858 voyage of the *Commodore* was considered one of the worst voyages ever. But it could have been worse. A lot worse.

Finally, we know what "yellow cake" is.

June 1999, BCF contracts its hamburger line out to a famous drive-in chain.

OPERATIONAL DELAYS—YOU CAN'T GET THERE FROM HERE

We've all heard the dreaded phrase: "Ferry delayed due to a mechanical issues." Apart from the three new German-built ferries (which seem to be tied to the dock much of the time), most of the ships are long past their "best before" date. So spare a thought to those grease-stained heroes under the car deck performing miracles with duct tape and bailing wire. They will get you to where you're going—eventually.

In 2010, BCF cancelled thirty-eight sailings due to mechanical failures ...

January 13, 2012, a fire party is mustered on the 31-year-old *Queen of Oak Bay* after smoke is found billowing from the engine-room.

Perhaps the reason you keep hearing those irritating car alarms going off during the voyage?

New onboard entertainment systems introduced in 2004 proved a welcome distraction to what was going on around you.

In 2005, BC Ferries was considering airport-style security, around the time the *Queen of Oak Bay* ran aground due to a missing cotter pin.

In 2006, BC Ferries bought a used ferry named the *John Atlantic Burr* and had it shipped out in pieces from Utah and reassembled in BC at over double the estimated cost.

GIL ISLAND

On March 22, 2006, while on its regular run from Prince Rupert to Port Hardy, the *Queen of the North* plowed into Gil Island in Wright Sound and sank. Sadly, two passengers never made it off the ship.

In 1997, the idea was floated of splitting the ferry system between the major routes and the smaller, less profitable Gulf Island routes.

As the fleet aged, engineers had to come up with more creative ways to keep vessels running.

A series of "hard landings" meant cancelled sailings while bent docks and battered ships were repaired.

In 2004, the Liberal government outraged BC shipbuilders by awarding contracts for three new super ferries to a German shipyard. The first arrived in 2007.

In 2008, electronic highway signs were installed at the approach to terminals to let passengers know at what time they wouldn't be going anywhere.

Shortly after announcing Wi-Fi on some routes in 2010, BC Ferries moved quickly to block "certain" websites, annoying "certain" passengers.

It was revealed that new life-saving procedures hadn't taken into account the disabled or infants.

An excellent idea. Sort of like having a restaurant non-smoking section inside the smoking section.

With a 2004 tugboat strike paralyzing the coastal forest industry, the ferries were some of the few vessels still sailing.

With the new ferries coming, what to do with the old ships? Not that there were lineups to buy them.

January 2007, the Nanaimo-Gabriola Island ferry made an unexpected departure from the dock while a resident's vehicle was still on the ramp, depositing the driver and his truck into the water. Fortunately, he was fished out unharmed, along with his truck.

BRIDGING THE GULF

The idea of a fixed link between Vancouver Island and the mainland has been around ever since the first ferry strike. A floating bridge, a suspension bridge, a tunnel, even a bridge/tunnel/floating bridge combination. Bridge detractors cite the loss of the unique island lifestyle, which would be destroyed by thousands of cars pouring across the bridge every day. This, of course, will never happen. If a bridge ever were built, for the times when the toll collectors weren't on strike, the toll would probably be ten times that of the current ferry fare.

Many Vancouver Islanders thought a bridge to the mainland would destroy the island's unique lifestyle.

Although some island lifestyles were more unique than others . . .

Each time the fleet was idled due to a labour disruption, or fares were raised, the idea of a bridge became more palatable to island residents.

But could a bridge and a ferry fleet co-exist?

And, more importantly, what would the bridge be called?

LABOUR VS. MANAGEMENT

Ferries management and the unions have always had a strange symbiotic relationship—like two wolverines tied up in a sack. Management intransigence and union demands have cost the economies of Vancouver Island and coastal communities dearly over the decades. Just the threat of a labour dispute sends visitors to Vancouver Island scurrying for the exits and a full-on strike inconveniences those who rely on the ferry system for doctors appointments, work, a trip to an Island bookstore to buy a Raeside cartoon collectio . . (that's enough! –ed.)

Following a strike at the Black Ball line that paralyzed ferry service between the mainland and Vancouver Island, the provincial government created BC Ferries in 1960. Passengers would never have to endure another ferry strike . . .

Ferry workers' salaries seemed pretty decent to the average British Columbian.

The Vancouver Island economy had the most to lose in any labour disruption.

The issue of contracting out was often at the center of ferry union grievances.

The numerous strikes not only eroded public support for their cause, unions also faced the threat of being legislated back to work

Regardless of how the strike ended, the damage had already been done.

Even something as trivial as uniforms could become a contentious issue.

Next year they'll be demanding 35 biscuits an hour and a squeaky toy allowance.

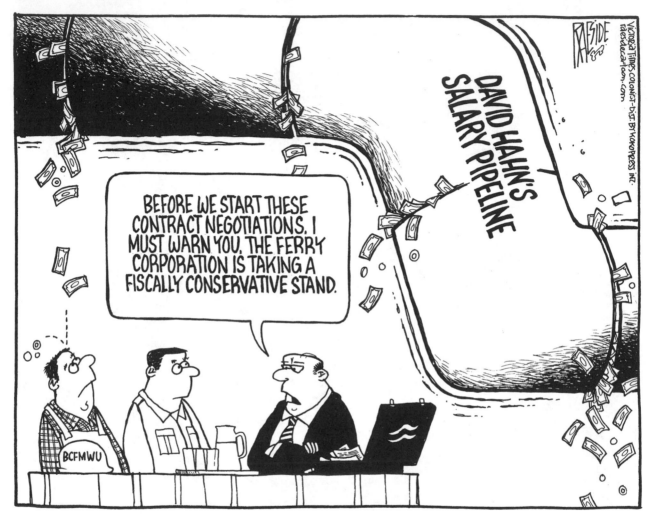

Bargaining with the union over salaries became a little trickier as executive compensation went through the roof.

Victoria Times Colonist—Dist. by KoKo Press Inc. www.raesidecartoon.com

FAST FERRIES
AND SLOW POLITICIANS

Politicians of all stripes cannot resist meddling with BC Ferries, often at their peril. Case in point: the Fast Ferries, or PacifiCats, which were the brainchild of then-premier Glen Clark, were supposed to revolutionize the way we crossed Georgia Strait. Built entirely of aluminum and using untested technology, the first vessel hit the water in 1988 and immediately everything went wrong. Besides the massive cost overruns during construction, they were cramped, stuffy, had no outside deck space and were limited in the number and size of vehicles they could carry. Unfortunately, the Fast Ferries were neither the first nor last case of political meddling that went awry on the BC Ferries file.

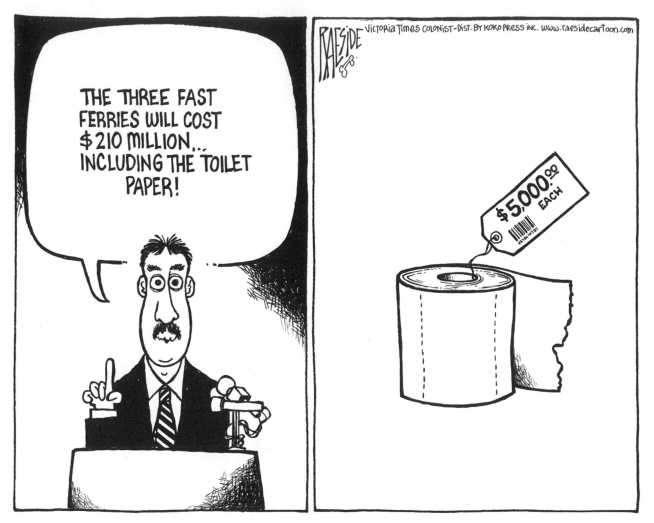

Then-premier Glen Clark's famous boast at the start of the PacifiCats Fast Ferries project. The final cost was actually over $450 million.

Pirates were seizing boats off the Mexican coast. Unfortunately, the increasingly unpopular PacifiCats weren't doing the Vancouver-Mazatlan run.

... and the wake thrown up by the PacifiCats was eroding valuable waterfront properties.

With costs mounting, would the government complete the remaining two PacifiCats? The answer was yes—a decision which played a large role in sinking the NDP government.

The bad news: BCF had no plans to raise the sunken *Queen of the North* ferry. The good news: the leaking fuel oil may kill the sea lice.

Everyone was catching 2010 Winter Olympics fever. Everyone, that is, except BC Ferries.

Not everyone had to pay to ride the ferries. Provincial MLAs each got a free ferry pass, although there was more chance you'd see them at the heliport than in a ferry lineup.

In 2000, the first suggestion of paid reservations was met with lukewarm response from the travelling public.

Unfortunately, none of my ideas made the cut.

Gambling was often suggested as a way to increase onboard revenues.

But with gambling comes the usual social problems . . .

Shock! Horror! Rumours of pot use by crew members!

But how would you know if they were stoned?

It worked for them when they sold BC Rail but kept the tracks.

In 2006, the feds came up with new rules regarding the discharge of raw sewage in coastal waters.

PRIVATIZATION

In what was supposed to be a brilliant move to keep BC Ferries at arms length from politics, and vice versa, the BC Ferry Corporation was converted to a "private corporation" in 2003. Although the corporation still requires generous cash infusions of public money, provincial transport ministers were sheltered from the fallout resulting from the numerous fare hikes and fuel surcharges. The privatization of the ferries does seem strange, considering BC Ferries was formed by the provincial government to prevent the travelling public from being held hostage by a private company . . . But with privatization came exciting changes: new terminals, new ships, new logos, new management compensation—and new fares to pay for it all.

It felt like British Columbians were losing ownership of their ferries.

The decision to award the contract to build three new ferries to a German shipyard infuriated the BC shipbuilding industry. Ferries brass and the government claimed local shipbuilders didn't have the expertise to build vessels of that size . . .

. . . the same government which touted BC expertise in shipbuilding to snag the federal contract to build icebreakers and other non-combat naval vessels.

With new improved ferry terminals came new and improved ways to spend your money.

Extreme makeover, BC Ferries-style.

BOWING TO PRESSURE, B.C. FERRIES PUTS PORTRAITS OF THE QUEEN BACK ON THE SHIPS.

Victoria Times Colonist · Dist. By kokopress inc. raesidecartoon.com

SEE THE PORTRAIT OF THE QUEEN $5.⁰⁰

ENTRANCE

February 2008, BCF decides to remove the portrait of the Queen from ships but quickly caved in the face of intense pressure from local monarchists and, presumably, their long-suffering corporate PR team.

Surcharges sneak their way onboard.

New terminals, new ships, new shops, same old waits . . .

. . . and same old excuses for fare increases.

With losses mounting, savings had to be found somewhere.

Although not at the executive level.

But passengers were fair game.

Details began to emerge on exactly how generous the CEO's compensation package was.

Time and again the taxpayer would bail the ferries out.

Always under threat from corporate bean counters, the Mill Bay ferry was one of the Island's most picturesque runs—and the cheapest.

And one of the deadest if BC Ferries bean counters had their way.

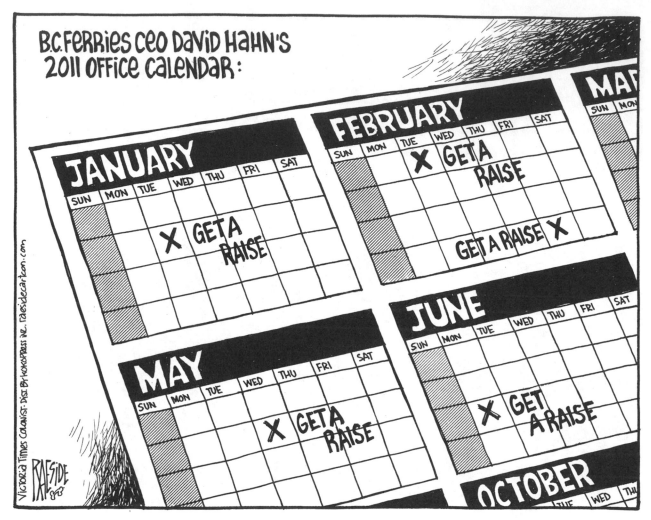

CEO salary increases became so regular, you could set your clock by them.

Once again, the board votes their CEO another pay raise.

December 2010, the corporation moves into a swanky new building in Victoria.

September 2011, David Hahn announces his retirement.

But what would, what *could* David Hahn do after he leaves the ferry corporation?

FARES

That whine you hear isn't coming from an overheated bearing in the engine of the *Queen of Gerontology*, it's coming from BC Ferries headquarters in Victoria, where management is justifying yet another fare hike.

It's not like you can drive up to the ticket booth and haggle over the price, or cross the street to take the competing ferry. Fuel surcharges seem to be the favourite way to wring more money out of passengers and each increase in crude oil prices sends ferry accountants scurrying for their calculators. There is a possibility the fleet will be converted to run on cheaper liquefied natural gas (LNG) meaning an end to the hated fuel surcharges—which will probably be replaced by LNG conversion surcharges.

Long considered a part of the designated provincial highway system, the ferry system has actually become a very expensive designated detour.

July 2011, BCF acquires a new state-of-the-art vessel simulator.

It was sometimes hard to know which drain your money was going down.

The smaller ferry runs always seemed to be hit the hardest by fare increases.

September 2005, after a recent minor earthquake, geoscientists estimate that Vancouver Island moved 5 millimetres to the west.

Like the airlines, BC Ferries became addicted to fuel surcharges.

And ferries CEO David Hahn's previous gig was in the aviation industry.

In 2008, in a clever promotion, a local Victoria supermarket introduced points that could be redeemable for ferry tickets.

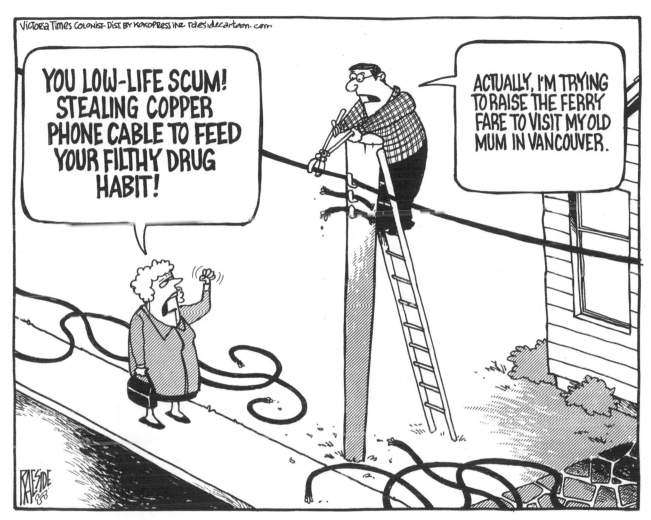

There were others who came up with more creative ways to pay for ferry travel.

Lower Mainland residents were moaning about proposed tolls for new bridges.

Fare increases seemed rapid and without warning.

Global oil prices dropped, fuel surcharges didn't.

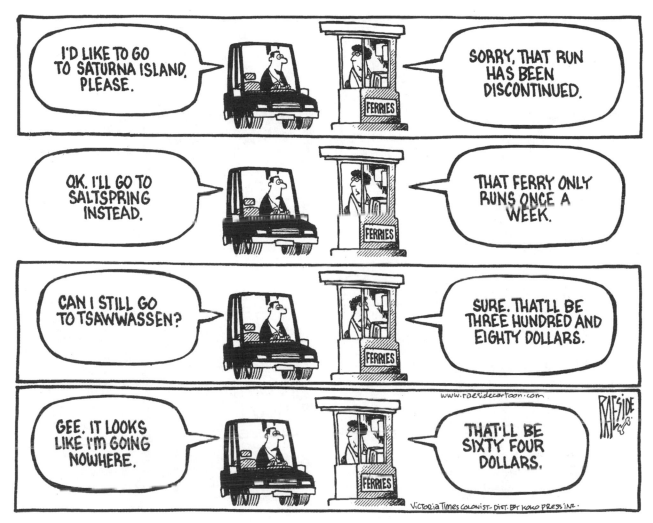

But you'll need to shell out $$ for a reservation to get there.

With global warming and rising sea levels, the Tsawwassen ferry terminal could end up under water—like ferry corporation finances.

Another good idea, bad timing . . .

The three certainties in life: death, taxes and fuel surcharges.

Sure, you'd have to endure a conga line on the pool deck and an annoying cruise director trying to get you to buy an onshore excursion package, but the food would be better.

Maybe there should be an ex-CEO surcharge.

December 2011, Mike Corrigan takes over as new CEO, inheriting a fleet of 35 ships and a boat-load of debt.

As fares rise, and passenger levels drop . . . whither BC Ferries?